Pebble Bilingual Books

Soy paciente/ I Am Patient

de/by
Sarah L. Schuette

Traducción/Translation
Martín Luis Guzmán Ferrer, Ph.D.

Capstone Press
Mankato, Minnesota

Pebble Bilingual Books are published by Capstone Press
151 Good Counsel Drive, P.O. Box 669, Mankato, Minnesota 56002
http://www.capstone-press.com

1 2 3 4 5 6 08 07 06 05 04 03

Library of Congress Cataloging-in-Publication Data
Schuette, Sarah L., 1976–
   [I am patient. Spanish & English]
   Soy paciente / de Sarah L. Schuette; traducción, Martín Luis Guzmán Ferrer =
I am patient / by Sarah L. Schuette; translation, Martín Luis Guzmán Ferrer.
   p. cm.—(Pebble bilingual books)
   Spanish and English.
   Includes index.
   Summary: Simple text and photographs show various ways children can be
patient.
   ISBN 0-7368-2304-2
   1. Patience—Juvenile literature. [1. Patience. 2. Spanish language materials—
Bilingual.] I. Title: I am patient. II. Title. III. Series: Pebble bilingual books.
BJ1533.P3S3818 2004
179'.9—dc21   2003004951

Editorial Credits
Mari C. Schuh and Martha E. H. Rustad, editors; Jennifer Schonborn, book designer
   and illustrator; Patrick Dentinger, cover production designer; Nancy White, photo
   stylist; Karen Risch, product planning editor; Eida Del Risco, Spanish copy editor;
   Gail Saunders-Smith, consulting editor; Madonna Murphy, Ph.D., Professor of
   Education, University of St. Francis, Joliet, Illinois, author of *Character Education in
   America's Blue Ribbon Schools*, consultant

Photo Credits
Capstone Press/Gary Sundermeyer, cover, 1, 4, 6, 8, 10, 20; Gregg Andersen, 12,
   14, 16, 18

Pebble Books thanks the Frederick family of North Mankato, Minnesota, for
modeling in this book. The author dedicates this book to her parents, Willmar and
Jane Schuette, Belle Plaine, Minnesota.

Table of Contents

Contenido

4

I am patient. I can wait calmly.

Yo soy paciente.
Sé esperar con calma.

I teach my friend to tie her shoes. I am patient as she learns.

Le enseño a mi amiga a atarse los zapatos. Soy paciente mientras ella aprende.

8

I listen quietly when
someone else is talking.
I wait for my turn to talk.

Escucho en silencio
cuando alguien está
hablando. Espero
mi turno para hablar.

I do not get angry when things go wrong. I try to fix them.

No me enojo cuando las cosas salen mal. Trato de arreglarlas.

I practice my
spelling words until
I know them better.
I keep trying.

Practico mis ejercicios
de ortografía para poder
aprender. Lo intento una
y otra vez.

I wait for my turn
to use the computer.

Espero mi turno para
usar la computadora.

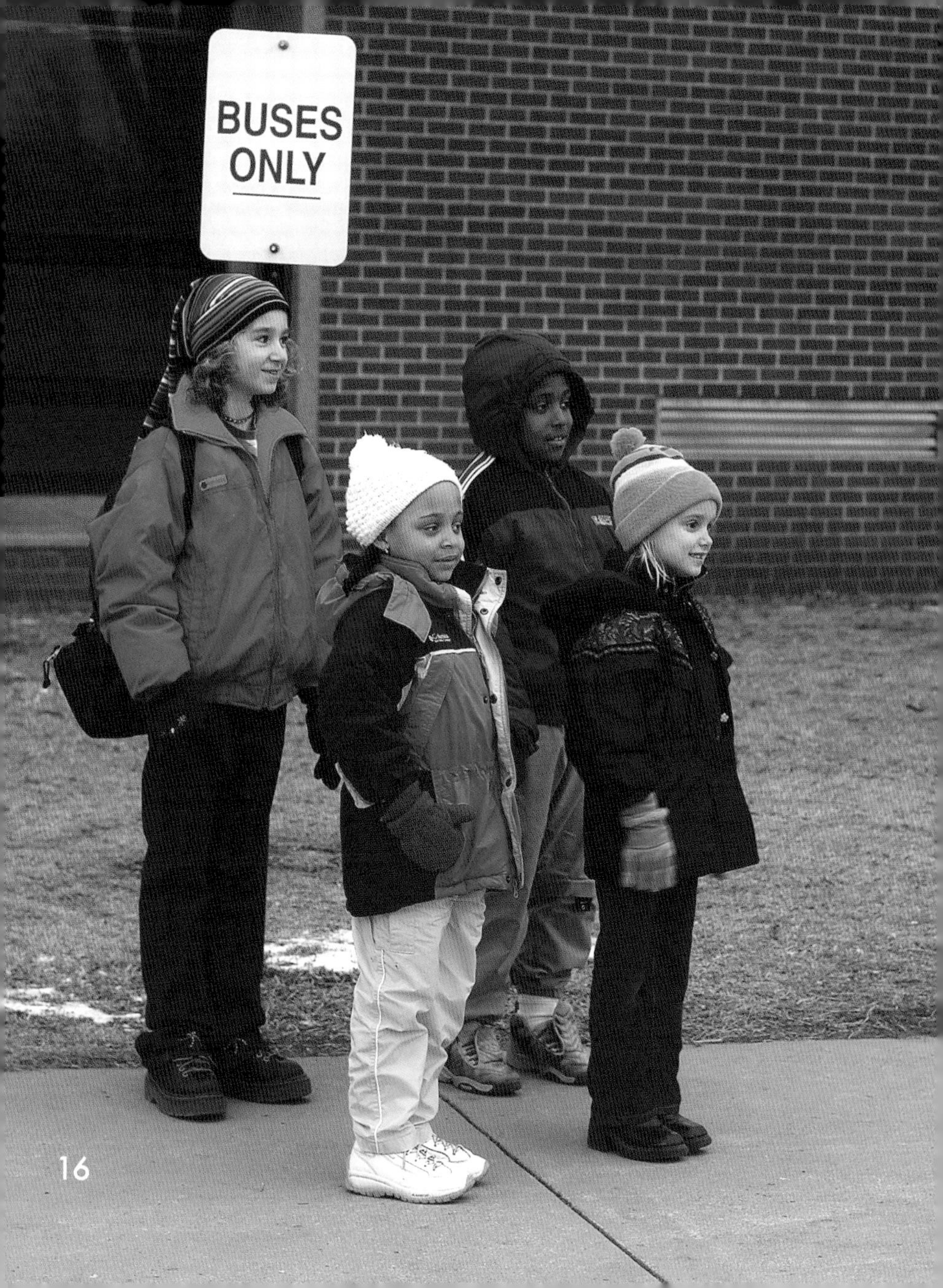
BUSES
ONLY

I wait patiently
for the bus.

Espero con paciencia
el autobús.

I wait to speak until
my teacher calls on me.

Espero mi turno para
hablar hasta que
el maestro me llama.

6 years
5 years
4 years

20

I am patient and calm.
I am not in a hurry. I
can wait.

Soy paciente y tranquila.
No tengo prisa.
Sé esperar.

Glossary

angry—wanting to argue or fight with someone

calm—quiet and peaceful; patient people are calm while they wait for something.

hurry—to do things as fast as you can

listen—to pay attention so that you can hear something; people who are patient listen quietly until it is their turn to talk.

patient—waiting calmly without complaining; patient people do not get angry or upset when things do not go as they expect.

practice—to keep working to improve a skill

wait—to stay in a place or do nothing for a long time until something happens; patient people can wait calmly.

Glosario

enojar—querer discutir o pelear con alguien

calmado—tranquilo y pacífico; las personas pacientes tiene calma mientras esperan.

prisa—hacer las cosa lo más rápido posible

escuchar—poner atención para poder oír las cosas; las personas pacientes escuchan en silencio hasta que es su turno de hablar.

paciente—esperar con calma sin quejarse; las personas pacientes no se enojan ni molestan cuando las cosas no resultan como lo esperan.

practicar—repetir una tarea para progresar

esperar—quedarse en un lugar o no hacer nada hasta que algo pasa; las personas pacientes esperan con calma.

Index

Índice